Looking For Love in All The Wrong Places

Beauty for Ashes

AIYAN BLEVINS

Looking For Love in All The Wrong Places - Beauty for Ashes

Cover design & editing by: Shana Washington

ISBN: 979-8-355-18999-0

Re-Store Outreach
Cedar Hill, TX
Reach us on the Internet: www.Re-storeoutreach.org

This Book Belongs to:

Contents

FORWARD

Bold, Brave, and Beautiful! "Looking For Love in All The Wrong Places – Beauty for Ashes" is that to say the very least. A story of a woman's discovery of self and her courage to face the demons that tried to steal her from destiny. This is a journey of healing that can only be told by Aiyan in her words, her way. A powerful reflection of truths that are not easily spoken, but Aiyan speaks to them with grace and Godly boldness.

Each chapter takes us on a journey and if we are honest, we can see ourselves. "Looking for love in all the wrong places-Beauty for Ashes" is an invitation to the readers. An invitation to search the dark places of our past. The places that we have held hostage because of fear and release them in the capable hands of our loving God.

In "Looking for Love in All the Wrong Places- Embracing God's Beauty for Ashes," Aiyan sacrifices her fears and her shame and allows God to use them as a catalyst to set captives free. This book shows us how God takes everything in our lives that went up in smoke and indeed gives us Beauty for Ashes, even if we were the ones who started the fire. Encounter this book with reverence, encounter this book with expectation, encounter this book ready to receive. You will be changed forever.

–Ikisha S. Cross

INTRODUCTION

The Lord is my light and my salvation; whom shall I fear? the Lord is the strength of my life; of whom shall I be afraid?

–Psalm 27:1

For years I feared the "what if?" What if people really knew the TRUTH? What if people knew my real struggle? What if people knew that I was struggling with the secrets of my past? What if people knew I had four children with five different baby daddies? What if people knew I was previously locked up? What if people knew I was molested by my babysitter? What if people knew I had been addicted to crack cocaine. What if people knew I was the town's "Harlot?" All the years I spent being afraid of people knowing my past stunted the growth of who I was becoming. All the low self-esteem, hurt, pain, shame, and guilt held me hostage to my fear instead of embracing the freedom that only Christ could bring. But now I am set free from everything that once held me back, and for that I am now made new.

I'm graced by God to share with other men and Women that God is a restorer, a healer, and a deliverer. Fear of rejection caused me to stay in places that I should've moved from long ago. Rebellion kept me in disobedience, but the Truth of God's love has set me free, and it can and will do the same for you.

The Spirit of the Lord God is upon me; because the Lord hath anointed me to preach good tidings unto the meek; he hath sent me to bind up the brokenhearted, to proclaim liberty to the captives, and the opening of the prison to them that are bound; 2. To proclaim the acceptable year of the Lord, and the day of vengeance of our God; to comfort all that mourn; 3. To appoint unto them that mourn in Zion, to give unto them beauty for ashes, the oil of joy for mourning, the garment of praise for the spirit of heaviness; that they might be called trees of righteousness, the planting of the Lord, that he might be glorified.

–Isaiah 61:1-3

HOW TO USE THIS BOOK

Therefore if any man be in Christ, he is a new creature: old things are passed away; behold, all things are become new.

–2 Corinthians 5:17-21

This is a journey to help you develop a more confident, hope-filled walk with you and God. This book aims to engage you in the process and possibilities of being made new. People who embrace positive change and are willing to move beyond what has been and embrace what shall be, will be successful.

As you read this book, I pray that you will be inspired, hear, feel, and live in your new beginning.

CHAPTER 1

IN THE BEGINNING

And I will be a father to you, And you shall be sons and daughters to Me, Says the Lord Almighty.

–2 Corinthians 6:18

Born and raised in a single parent household, my mother taught me the ways of the Lord. She raised me with the belief that God was all that I ever needed. She instilled morals, values, love, respect, honor in me. She taught me that He would never leave me nor forsake me (Hebrews 13:5). She also taught me that no matter what, God would always love me. I was taught that God was a Good Father. My Mother made sure that I attended church, Sunday school, Baptist Training Union, Wednesday night prayer meetings, choir rehearsal, and so many other things. I was filled with gratitude, but I felt something was missing.

My Mother was big on faith in God and morals. She taught me to never give people something to talk about. As children, my brother and I were not allowed to do things that other children were able to do. We had rules, chores and she taught us responsibility. As early as I can remember, I saw what it was for a mother to raise children on her own. I remember my mom always carried the load by herself. I quickly realized it was normal to see mothers raising children on their own. My mother gave me all she knew to give.

I had a great upbringing, but I always felt like I was missing something that every child needs. I was missing a father. I had no father to teach me what love from a man looked like. I had no earthly father to teach me how a man should treat me, love me, respect me, or how I should respect myself. I had no father to teach me how not to be taken advantage of by men or how to accept a compliment with no strings attached.

There are just some things that only a father can teach his daughter about men. A girl needs to know the characteristics of a good man as well as the type of man to run from and not to like the manipulator, cheater, self-centered, unreliable, and dishonest man. How could I have expected my earthly father to warn me of these types of men when he possessed some of those characteristics.

My father was considered "The Man" who lived in the same town as my mother. Even with him living near us, my mother was left alone to raise two children all by herself. Although I felt my father should have shown me love, he really wasn't able to give me that kind of love. He knew how to say I love you but was not able to show it through his actions. My father wasn't shown love, so the cycle repeated itself.

My parents divorced when I was 2 years old and as a result, I have no memory of living with my father. I have no childhood memories of my father giving me Christmas gifts, birthday gifts, or attending school functions. I have no childhood memories of my father leading, nurturing, or molding me. I don't remember him ever pursuing to spend time with me.

Daddy loved me with what he knew. I will always remember me being the one to chase my daddy's love. The example of seeing daddy provide for his family, loving his children, embracing mommy, or spending quality time with his family was something I never experienced with my father. Most of the time when I saw my father it was because I pursued him, not because he pursued me.

My great-grandmother would watch us while my mom worked, guess who lived across the street? My dad! As soon as mom would go to work the whistle at her nearby job would blow. That was an indicator that mom was at work and on the clock because she was never late. Knowing that mom was at work I would immediately run over to my dad's house. I had more freedom with my dad because he wasn't as strict as my mom, but I was looking for a father's love, not freedom. As a child, I thought just being in his presence was enough for me. Every time my dad opened the door, acted silly, and made me laugh; I identified that as love. That was what he knew to give me.

REFLECTIONS

Forgiving someone, especially a parent, is probably the hardest thing there is. But if you want emotional and spiritual freedom, forgiveness is the key to unlocking what you most deeply desire.

What is the worst thing that can happen if you choose to forgive your parent(s)?

How has holding on to the hurt hindered you?

What does it mean to you that God is your Heavenly Father?

CHAPTER 2

IF REBELLION WAS A PERSON

I will instruct you and teach you in the way you should go; I will counsel you with my loving eye on you.

–Psalms 32:8 (NIV)

As I breezed through my elementary years and time went on, at the beginning of 6th grade my mother remarried and we moved away from the small town where my biological father lived. We moved to the big city of Ft. Worth, Texas. My rebellion journey quickly began in middle school. I would spend my time at school talking back to teachers and seeking attention as the class clown so I could be seen and feel heard.

Alcohol and marijuana were my preference over high school once I was introduced to them. I was a follower just so I could be accepted but I became a flunky and a stooge just for laughs and giggles. As the class clown, getting kicked out of class and getting suspended from school was a normal routine. After exhausting my school principal, I was sent to the Student Referral Center across town making it difficult for my mother on her job. She would have to be late for work, just to ensure that I was at the center, to continue receiving my education. Today I Thank God for covering and protecting my mother's position.

My mother believed in discipline, and I was fully aware of the consequences, but I was willing to do anything to receive the love I was craving. You see, acting out got me attention. Rebelling continued throughout high school but worse because I started sneaking out of the house at night and stealing my stepfather's company car. I lied, stole, and did whatever I wanted to do. I did all the things my mother spoke against like sex before marriage, drugs, and disrespect.

Desiring now to be loved by a male, I gave my virginity away at sixteen to my oldest daughter's father. I continued sneaking out of the house until I was eventually caught but it didn't stop me. I continued to sneak out the house in the middle of the night. He would bring me back in time to get ready for school. He would even pick me up during school and drop me off so I could catch the bus home as if I had been at school all day.

Every time I skipped school, I would try to make it home to erase the answering machine so mom would never receive the call from my teachers about my behavior. Eventually she found out. She would whoop me, ground me, threaten me with a girl's home or psychiatrist. Nothing worked because by now the seed of disobedience had fully manifested by the age of sixteen. I was rebellious and out of control, but my mom did all she knew to do.

During 10th grade, my stepfather received a promotion and we moved to Memphis, TN. where my rebellion continued. I was enrolled in a new school, and it wasn't long before I identified with the crowd that I wanted to follow. Being a follower got me attention, I was recognized, not knowing all along I was being made a fool of, by myself and my peers.

Not being phased by being in an unknown place I continued skipping school, stealing my parent's car, and *looking for love in all the wrong places.* I would sneak out and sneak boys in on occasions. I knew the consequences, but it didn't matter. I was willing to go to extreme lengths to get what I wanted and was willing to pay the price. I was on a search to be loved and I was determined to find it.

After enrolling in high school in Memphis, Tn. I soon found the guy whom I thought I loved. Looking back, I realized I was too young to even know what love was. I got pregnant by him while we were still in high school but out of fear of what my mother would think, we had an abortion only to later get pregnant by him again and had my first-born son.

I can remember it like it was yesterday. His father was still in high school, and I had graduated. While pregnant I encountered the cycle of rejection by my son's father after he left me barefoot and pregnant in his mother's home. He moved out across town, enrolled in a new school, and began seeing another girl. Eventually he dropped out of school and began a life as a drug dealer, got shot in the club, and later found himself in a federal prison. All of this was going on while I was left alone to carry his and my first child. Creating yet another cycle of rejection that my child would also have to break.

After my son Justin was born and my 6-weeks checkup was complete, I moved back to Texas and resided with my great- grandmother, where I continued *looking for love*. My grandmother lived in the same town as my father. It never mattered to me that my dad didn't help to raise me, nor did it matter that my father didn't pursue me while in Memphis. I always gravitated to him because I wanted to know a father's love. I was so happy to see my father again! At that point, I had given myself to several boyfriends but still never experienced love.

Whether you are a son or daughter there needs to be some type of example in your life of what singleness really looks like and knowing that it's okay to be single. If it's marriage, there needs to be a Godly example of what marriage should be and what motherhood and fatherhood should be like.

As we know sometimes things don't work out as God has planned for us. He ordains marriage! Sex outside of marriage is out of God's will and his original plan for parenting. Although things happen, a daughter needs to know from her father/mother the things to be aware of in a man, both the good and the bad. A son also needs to know what good and bad qualities to look for in a woman.

Often, it's not that our parents don't desire to give this to us, but how they can give what they weren't given and what they don't understand? That is beyond me but it's not beyond God. A girl's first love should be a father's love. A boy's first love should be from his mother's love and ultimately the love should be given from both parents. When your parents don't give you the love you desire and need you look somewhere else.

REFLECTIONS

Why do you think a parent's love is important?

How did your parents show their love for you?

How does God show you, his love?

CHAPTER 3

THE SEARCH STILL LEADS TO REJECTION

Flee from sexual immorality. All other sins a man commits are outside his body, but he who sins sexually sins against his own body.

–1 Corinthians 6:18 (NIV)

Still searching for love I found my best friend from high school and headed for Ft. Worth. I would leave my grandmother's house with my baby and stay the weekend with her and her mom. Eventually after a couple of visits I was introduced to her cousin; my second son's father. Eventually I moved to Ft. Worth and stayed with my son's father and mother to continue embracing the cycle of being attracted to another man with no job, no independence, unreliable and a daily drinker. It was a constant back and forth trip to Ft. Worth. We would break up and get back together. I moved back in with my granny after becoming pregnant with a second child. After I had my second son, I applied for housing and moved.

My son's father denied him until the blood test proved what we both already knew. YOU ARE THE FATHER! With little to no support at all, the relationship eventually ended with me repeating the cycle with a second child, different father, but the same rejection. It was obvious that I was comfortable with the cycle of dysfunction and rejection, but the search for love continued.

At this point in my life and with all my experience, I thought I was more aware of what I did and didn't want from a man. I began seeing other guys and even though it didn't work, my search was not over. I was determined to find someone to love me.

After living in Cleburne, TX. for quite some time, I backed tracked and got involved with a guy I knew I should've stayed away from. I fell for the things he was doing for me and my two sons. It wasn't much, but to me it was everything since I never received gifts or attention from the one man that should have given it in the beginning- my father. I simply didn't know what to expect, accept, allow, or even where to begin and end. Again, the cycles repeated.

BOOM! My doors were kicked in by the police. Apparently, they received a tip that the guy I had no business backtracking to was at my house and they were looking for him. They found drugs in my place, so I was charged with possession of a controlled substance. On top of all that, I was handcuffed and charged right in front of my one- and two-year-old sons. Yeah, he was a drug dealer, but I measured his for me by all the possessions and there was no end to what I equated love to be.

Even though I knew his lifestyle, he was popular, and wanted by the ladies but he was with me. As if getting bailed out by my mother who taught me better wasn't bad enough, I had to move back in with my grandmother because I lost my house. With him getting incarcerated, the craving for love continued.

Out of sight out of mind I continued to go backwards had sexual encounters with what I thought was my first love because we had connection from giving him my virginity at sixteen. He was married at this time, but our friendship continued over the years. No matter what, he always pursued me and that was the feeling I wanted from my dad…to be pursued.

Pregnant with my third child Jamaureee, I didn't know if her father was the married man or the one in prison. After giving birth to my daughter, I gave her the last name of the man I found out later wasn't her father. At that point in my life, I was consumed with embarrassment, guilt, and shame and felt like my life was just a big blob.

REFLECTIONS

What choices have you made that kept that part of you or your life on repeat?

How did you or how can you end that unhealthy cycle?

How can you forgive and still love yourself throughout this process?

CHAPTER 4

I THOUGHT I WAS GOOD

If you think you are standing strong, be careful not to fall.

– 1 Corinthians 10:12 (NLT)

And there I was, a single mother with three children and four different fathers. I know that math may seem off, but remember I mentioned my daughter having the wrong man's last name. I didn't receive support from any of them. I did what I knew to do from watching my mother raise me and my brother. I stopped expecting their fathers to help and relied on my own abilities and the help that God always provided, even during my poor decision making. I continued to work and do the best I could on my own.

Eventually I got a decent job, a car, and slowed down enough to get my own house with help from my mom and granny. Guess who furnished my living room, Dear old dad. Thank you, Daddy! It was the first gift that I can recall receiving from him. Of course, my stepmom played a significant role in that and many other situations. I will always be grateful to her for that.

At this point in my life, I was in and out of church seeking strength in Sunday school but not putting in the time to get to know God on my own. I went through the motions in life and believed the lie that I told myself – Aiyan, you are ok. Attending church is how I camouflaged the pain and mimicked what I saw. I merely let the God that my mom knew, and the preacher talked about carry me.

The kids were growing and doing well in school. There were no complaints, no worries, I would say we were living a "good life". I was still chasing love; I just camouflaged it a little better. I joined the choir, and the kids were in the children's choir. I played it off, but I was dying on the inside.

I was not in a place in my life where I could hear God's voice and deal with my internal problems. I knew the God that mom spoke of, but I never gave Him the opportunity to be my Heavenly Father. The only example that I had of a father was the one I pursued that never pursued me. So, I expected God "The Father" to brush me off just like my father did. My father would embrace me when he saw me, but it was only because of me always chasing him for love.

I was afraid to tell someone what I was dealing with out of fear of being judged. I overlooked how I already revealed my internal battles to the world by the choices I had made. I was the church woman on Sundays and Wednesdays, but on Fridays and Saturdays, I found babysitters and hit the streets hoping to run into Mr. Right. I always made sure I went back to God on those two days until all the pretending came to an end because my cover was blown.

Without a solid foundation of your own in Christ, you will surely drift away when the storms of life hit you. I know this all too well because a new sheriff came into town. I was introduced to him, and he changed my life and lifestyle. What I thought was a hit and miss became an addiction that took me from Motherhood to Another Hood! By the way, his first name was Crack, Crack Cocaine.

REFLECTIONS

What addiction changed your life? Was it drugs or alcohol? Maybe something less obvious like social media for the likes or food for comfort?

How did that addiction change your life?

What have you learned about yourself from that addiction?

CHAPTER 5

UP IN SMOKE

For the world offers only a craving for everything we see, and pride in our achievements and possessions. These are not from the Father, but are from this world.

– 1 John 2:16 (NLT)

And just like that, I was hooked.

So many dysfunctional cycles of poor choices of men I kept finding my way in. Looking for love I thought I found it in Mr. Crack Cocaine and after just a few hits, I became addicted. I didn't understand because I wasn't looking for the high; I was looking for the love and acceptance I felt the high gave me. I thought that it was something I could double-dutch my way in and out of. I thought I could use it to cover up and medicate all my feelings of being a failure and a nobody with three children by three different men. I thought it would fill the void of feeling empty inside with no man to love me or my babies.

During all the searching for love and finding Mr. Crack Cocaine, I couldn't hold a job or be a mother to my children. I became a thief, a liar, and the town's harlot just to support my addiction. I found a safe place to get high. My dad's house. He too was an addict. Dad would allow me to get high with him, bring him dope and help him destroy the both of us. I guess he thought he was doing the right thing.

More times than I can count, I exchanged sexual favors for drugs with men who came to my daddy's house because they knew what I would do for a hit. For some reason I thought my dad would protect me, but I didn't realize I was pouring salt on open wounds. My dad simply couldn't give me what I was looking for…LOVE, GUIDANCE, PROTECTION and DIRECTION.

So many days and even weeks I would be gone from home, leaving my children with their elderly great-grandmother so I could chase the next high. As if crack wasn't enough, I became an IV drug user. My life was so far out of control to the point of no return I thought I would die with a crack pipe in my mouth. I have faced death numerous times with guns pulled to my head for failure to produce sexual favors that I promised men in exchange for drugs. I found myself in legal trouble, locked up and placed on probation.

I was an addict, and my addiction controlled my mind, body, and soul. Since I was unable to live out and complete the stipulations of probation, my children were forced to be placed in separate homes while I was sent to SAFPF (Substance Abuse Felony Punishment Facility). SAFPF was a program that helped people get their life in order. It reiterated staying clean, making healthy choices, having good work ethics…all the things my mother instilled in me.

There was just one thing SAFPF couldn't help me with, looking for love in all the wrong places. I knew not to get involved with anyone that used drugs, but keep in mind it was at all costs. I had to deal with the pain of how my poor choices led me to where I was. I had to face the fact that my children were being raised by my mom and my elderly great-grandmother. All this time God was protecting my babies because I couldn't.

I finally graduated from SAFPF and was released to the Freeman Center halfway house in Waco, TX. I was able to get weekend passes and visits from people like my boyfriend at the time. Let's call him Mr. Diamond. We even snuck in a sexual encounter on one of those visits, but I will get to that in a second. I completed my program, aftercare program, and was well on my way to full recovery.

Finally, I'm free!

I got home, I got a job at my local newspaper, and I got back into church…well technically I got back into the building but still mimicked others. The best part was I got to be with my kids again and spend time with my boyfriend who stayed down with me while I was locked up. He even presented me with my first diamond when I got out.

I never questioned his loyalty, but that was a mistake. How could a ring mean that much to me? I mean no one ever thought enough about me or loved me to the point of giving me a ring. I had no idea it was a cover up from all the cheating he did while I was locked up. That was a hard way to learn why not to equate love with possessions.

Of course, the story didn't end there. I found out I was pregnant. AGAIN! Another child, another cheater, another liar, another dysfunctional relationship. Soon enough my daughter Edboni would be born.

REFLECTIONS

What bad habits have you been holding on to?

Choose one bad habit and write down how your life would be different if you replaced that habit with a better one.

What good habit can you start today to remove the bad habit?

CHAPTER 6

I WILL HELP YOU GOD

and human hands can't serve his needs—for he has no needs. He himself gives life and breath to everything, and he satisfies every need.

– Acts 17:25 NLT

It was history in the making, a world record! My relationship with Mr. Diamond lasted four long years. All the women wanted him, but he was all mine. At least that's what I believed. There I was on baby number four and another cycle of cheating, lies and rejection. I was so disgusted with myself! Bad choices one after another and I was sick of myself.

While my children and I were living with my grandmother, I would go to his house at night to see him, lay with him, get dressed up and hit the scene at the Cafe, the neighborhood spot. I thought it was love but it was dysfunction wrapped in a bow.

I was so sick of myself and what I accepted; I returned to Mr. Crack Cocaine. After all, at least I knew it was all for the thrill of the moment. Mr. Crack Cocaine was my homie, my lover, and my friend. I thought it was all I needed and cared about. For more than 15 years, I experienced relapse after relapse. I found myself in too deep with no way out but eventually, I got it together. I couldn't explain how I got out of it but now I know it was Jesus – My Good Good Father.

Seven years later, I was still clean. I moved into my own apartment and cut it off with baby daddy #4. I was a walking ball of pain, shame, and disappointment, but not enough to stop me from continuing my search. I was determined to find love.

I had a close friend and neighbor of mine who wanted to introduce me to her uncle who was coming to town. We started talking on the phone and he seemed like a nice guy. Still searching for love and being in a vulnerable place, I jumped in headfirst with him. We immediately started spending time together when he came to town. I ignored every sign the Holy Spirit gave me. To be honest I had no idea what it felt like to encounter the Holy Spirit so I couldn't recognize that nudge or intuition. God was speaking, but I had selective hearing.

By now my rejection and the beautiful picture that Satan had painted was a Masterpiece of beautiful lies. I was so blind in my search for love. He told me he was a minister of the Gospel, and I believed him. He had a good job, his own business, and he was a man of God. He was hard working, a provider, and a husband. So, we got married! I was so desperate and tired of searching for the kind of love that only God could give me.

Behind every detailed prayer and scripture was nothing but deception in a suit. He was a con artist, a liar, a cheat. I had no idea I was his 5th wife or that he had been to prison for practicing law without a license. Did I mention he was addicted to crack cocaine? This man caused me nothing but pain, but at least I could blame him for my self-inflicted wounds. The root of it all was rejection.

My husband had just been ordained as a minister. When everything came out in the opening, he had been having an affair with my choir director. I remember running into the pastor's study to tell him that he had ordained a demon. I cried out to the Lord and asked why he would allow me to embarrass myself. I was humiliated and had to deal with all the stares and whispers in the church. All of this and when all I ever wanted was to know a father's love.

A co-worker gave me a bible and I began reading scripture on bitterness, marriage, and forgiveness. I began seeking God for myself. Today I understand that God didn't let all these things happen because he didn't love me, but it was the beginning of understanding God's love. It was the beginning of understanding and obeying his voice. How do you obey what you don't understand? The type of love that I had spent most of my life seeking after could only be found in God.

I never sat long enough to identify God's love because I didn't know him as Father. I never knew that God would be all that I needed. I only knew God through my mother's eyes. I knew enough to know that I could find the answer in God's word, but I didn't want to do the work because God was a spirit, and I needed a tangible love. I didn't know that God's love was tangible too.

There were limitations to God, and I needed the touch of a physical man. I needed to physically be shown love. Why would this God pursue a woman like me? I thought I was helping God by marrying someone who said he was a man of God. Surely a man of God wouldn’t let me down. I was so embarrassed and confused! I was consumed with shame from having four children with four different men and now a cheating, drug addict, lying, and abusive husband.

Even after knowing that adultery was grounds for divorce, I remained because I didn’t want to give up on God. I was reading his Word and believed that he could restore us. So, I tried again and again but bitterness settled in.

I left the choir, and my husband was sat down from his role in ministry. I couldn't stand to hear him pray and the abuse in the home was bad, but I tried to cover up and pretend nothing was going on. My husband continued to be dishonest in and out of the church. He eventually moved us to another church to hide from what transpired but the whole town already knew.

One Wednesday night after prayer service, I returned home to discover my husband trying to camouflage his crack addiction as an asthma attack. I ended up relapsing with my husband that very night. After 7 years of sobriety, I fell into temptation with my husband, the Minster of the Gospel. Eventually things spiraled so far out of control that we separated, I moved, and had once again awakened the demon. This time it wasn't just one.

REFLECTIONS

How do you see yourself? Why?

How do you want to see yourself?

How do you think God sees you? Why?

CHAPTER 7

THE CYCLE CONTINUES

I don't really understand myself, for I want to do what is right, but I don't do it. Instead, I do what I hate.

– Romans 7:15 (NLT)

The demons were awakened the moment I relapsed and put the pipe back in my mouth. I had moved into an apartment on the east side of my hometown where I tried to function and failed. There are what society calls functioning addicts – those with addictions that can hold down while maintaining a family. However, I was not a functioning addict. My addiction was exposed to the public. I tried working and being a mom, but my addiction had the best of me.

One day I gave a friend a ride to Ft. Worth, TX, and next thing I knew, a year had passed, and I was still out there on a drug spree. After my life continued to spiral out of control, my children were once again placed with family and friends. Holidays and birthdays had passed but I was too high to try to see my children or make sure any of their needs were met. I was so far gone; I missed a court date and my oldest daughter's father was given custody.

I finally returned to Cleburne thanks to my eldest sister who picked me up and took me home. After being gone for a year, I had lost everything. I lost my apartment. I lost the relationship with my children. I lost the woman I had worked so hard to become.

By the grace of God, my Aunt Bert opened her heart and her home to me. She knew I was still struggling, but she wanted to see me do better. One day I was lying in a bed in a crack house when I heard the voice of someone say, “Donneye didn’t make it.” I used to bob and weave through my addiction, but it came to a very dark end when I lost my youngest sister to breast cancer.

I had the hardest time forgiving myself for hurting those close to me and not being there for my sister and my children when they needed me most. I especially let my mother down and couldn't see myself as anything but a failure. So, I chose to stay with my addiction. I had two monkeys on my back, crack cocaine and unforgiveness. Due to my choices and often self-inflicted trauma, I couldn’t get past myself or my bad decisions.

For the next few months, I continued to battle with my addiction. My cousin who lived in Dallas would try to convince me to move with her. Every time I said yes, she would come to pick me up and catch me with my addiction in my hand walking to my father’s house. I would stand there, take that hit, and refuse to go. She kept coming back. She was so persistent and continued to dance back and forth with me until I surrendered. I saw God's tangible love at that moment. I was finally sick and tired of cycles and self-inflicting pain due to my poor decisions. The day I finally accepted her offer; I received her as the help God had sent my way. I moved to Dallas where I continued to look for love in all the wrong places.

REFLECTIONS

Have you ever felt like you were stuck in a never-ending cycle? If so, how did you get out of it, or what changes did you make to not feel stuck?

If you haven't gotten out of it yet, pray about it and ask God for direction. In the space below write down what God spoke to you.

CHAPTER 8

REJECTION GOT A HOLD ON ME

Oh yes, you shaped me first inside, then out; you formed me in my mother's womb. I thank you, High God—you're breathtaking! Body and soul, I am marvelously made! I worship in adoration—what a creation! You know me inside and out, you know every bone in my body; You know exactly how I was made, bit by bit, how I was sculpted from nothing into something. Like an open book, you watched me grow from conception to birth; all the stages of my life were spread out before you, The days of my life all prepared before I'd even lived one day.

– Psalms 139:13-16 MSG

I lived in fear, I spoke in fear, I responded in fear. Every decision I made was based on rejection and fear. I passed up many opportunities because I didn't believe in myself. I didn't view myself from a healthy perspective. I saw myself as a failure. I used to allow others to put me down or I would beat them to the punch out of fearing rejection. I agreed with who people said I was and what my experience made me believe I was. I really didn't see myself in any other way.

For years fear tormented me. I was afraid to apply for certain jobs out of fear of being rejected. I became comfortable pretending to be someone I wasn't. I continued to pretend everything was okay while dying on the inside. I even feared that God would reject me. Afterall, why would he pursue me when no one else ever did. It was always me chasing after love. I feared all the what ifs, so I hid. Every disagreement, misunderstanding, and conversation was based on fear.

Although I was delivered from crack cocaine, I had wounds that were cut deep. I turned into a people pleaser always seeking validation from others while still searching to be accepted and loved. I even started to live my life based on the opinions of others. Not loving myself, seeing myself, or knowing my worth left me struggling with unforgiveness and an identity crisis.

The move to Dallas changed my life. I was finally delivered from crack cocaine and have been clean since 2007. The bad marriage, the incarceration, choosing crack cocaine over my family, and letting my children down were failures and bad choices I believed I couldn't be delivered from. For years I sat in a wounded place. I found myself always trying to fit into places that I wasn't created to be in. I was meant to be who God created me to be and on my 50th birthday, I finally woke up. On July 16, 2020, I started looking for love in all the right places. The only place. In God's presence.

REFLECTIONS

Think of a time you tried to fit in instead of standing out. What or who were you hiding yourself from? Why do you think that is?

CHAPTER 9

I FOUND HIS VOICE

He let you hear his voice from heaven so he could instruct you. He let you see his great fire here on earth so He could speak to you from it.

– Deuteronomy 4:36

FEAR…ANXIETY… UNBELIEF…

The pandemic hit the world in a wave and left people lost. Everything was shut down and doors were closed…even the church. Some churches were streaming live, and some weren't. We were pushed to seek God for ourselves. It was a time to come out of a familiar place of a "church building" and rise to be the church. We were called to be the body of Christ. I took this opportunity to clearly see how far I had come and the journey I still needed to take.

I had accepted the Lord Jesus Christ as my Savior long ago, but I wasn't living out what I confessed. I was still going through the motions of looking the part and having a form of godliness but denied the power. There was one foot in and one foot out of the door. Even after being delivered from my addiction, I still found myself in the clubs, drinking, smoking weed, and up Sunday morning at church. I was creating events, standing as an usher, a worship singer, speaking the word while still so far from living it.

For far too long, I depended on the voice of others to hear from God. I wanted and needed a relationship with God for myself. I didn't realize it then but now I know there was a problem if I only heard from God through others. While God does often speak through people, it's important to understand He will speak to circumstances and wounds from our trauma. For so long I believed the church building was the only place I could encounter God's presence. I didn't have to fake it until I made it. I had received and heard the word, but I neglected to produce it because I truly believe that I didn't really know him for myself.

I began following a ministry on social media and listening to live videos when I clearly heard God tell me to "come out and trust me." I was afraid because when I heard that I knew it was God speaking to me through someone who never met me or knew what I was in search of. All the hype of church protocol and following the order of the systems put in place were just a camouflage looking like the Holy Spirit.

I wanted and needed to be healed and made whole. I had so many wounds I had suppressed so much that they weren't wounds; they just grew to be a part of me. I confessed, "God I want to get to know you for myself." At that point I joined a church and was a member for 7+ years where I grew so much as a person. One day I just stopped growing. Deep down inside I knew there had to be more. I had to be honest with God concerning where I was spiritually. The experience of the pandemic led me to a relationship with God. When I heard his voice, it led me to his love.

REFLECTIONS

Have you ever prayed about something and received confirmation through someone else? If so, what was it?

Sometimes we only go to God for the big decisions, if we go to Him at all. What are some smaller decisions you need to make? Write them down below. I challenge you to take them to God before you make decisions and wait to hear from Him.

CHAPTER 10

A FATHER'S LOVE

Love is patient and kind. Love is not jealous or boastful or proud or rude. It does not demand its own way. It is not irritable, and it keeps no record of being wronged. It does not rejoice about injustice but rejoices whenever the truth wins out. Love never gives up, never loses faith, is always hopeful, and endures through every circumstance.

– 1 Corinthians 13:4-7(NLT)

I found love. I found a father's love. I found God the Father, God the Son, and God the Holy Spirit love that was with me that entire time. I found his voice, his correction, his instruction, and his character through his Holy Word. I found that God the Father has always been for me, and that no poor decision would ever cause him to stop loving me.

When he created me, he was fully aware of what I would encounter and that I would return to the Father's Love. For He knows the plans he has for me, and for you.

Everything I went through and put myself through worked out. My life and everything I overcame was by the grace of God. You too can overcome your struggles. He already knew my beginning and end, yet he loved me. Nothing gets past him. He knew the very day that I would find his love and run back to him. And guess what? His arms were opened wide to receive me. And guess what else? His arms are open wide waiting for you so you can find how he loves you.

What I heard throughout the years wasn't my conscience but my helper. I entered a relationship with "The Father." I've learned so many amazing things about the Father and myself. The Holy Spirit was my guide, but numerous years were spent in rebellion, because I didn't recognize the voice. God says my sheep know my voice and a stranger they won't follow. I was never an orphan without love from my father. All those years I spent wandering, chasing, looking, and searching for what was there all along…A Father's Love.

All the things I wanted from my earthly father that he didn't know how to give, I found in my Heavenly Father. His voice led me to His love. I continue seeking God and overcoming fears of being different but unique. I've learned to understand that my bad choices, failures, and trauma could never annul his love for me. I haven't stopped following His voice since.

I left a comfortable and familiar place to join a Prophetic Ministry Truth Church in Cleburne under the leadership of my Senior servants and Pastors, Apostle Kirkland and Prophet Ikisha Cross. Hearing His voice led me to a relationship and surrendering to a father that loves me with an everlasting love. I have grown to identify how God speaks to me and I'm overcoming fears, rejection, and wounds from my past.

Today I know my past is full of bad experiences and choices, but none of them identify who I am. I am fearless, I am chosen, and I am called by God. The truth of God's word continues to heal me. I am now able to love my father, forgive myself, and walk in forgiveness of others. My father has been delivered from his addiction and I can honestly say I love him. I am blessed to have four amazing children, eleven grandchildren, and an amazing husband of four years.

I'm growing to see myself as God sees me. My past no longer dictates my future. My future is controlled by my Heavenly Father and his promises are mine because I believe so. I no longer chase after love because his love for me stands forever. I am still under construction, but I am no longer struggling to find my identity. The journey isn’t perfect, but I am no longer seated in shame, guilt, or fear. I’m knocking down every lie that is revealed or tries to creep up. I'm grateful for His love, His patience, and His kindness. God is and has always been my protector, my provider and my hope to stay in the race. I'm embracing the truth of who God says I am.

He's been a GOOD GOOD FATHER!

CHAPTER 11

BECAUSE GOD SAID SO

The Lord directs the steps of the godly. He delights in every detail of their lives. Though they stumble, they will never fall, for the Lord holds them by the hand.

– Psalm 37:23-24 (NIV)

BECAUSE GOD SAID SO, I have chosen to partner with who he says I am. I now have the courage to knock down every lie that tells me all that I am not. I am choosing to agree with the truth of God's word that tells me I am not my experiences. It is a truth that tells me I can do all things through Christ who gives me strength (Philippians 4:13 NIV). This truth tells me that healing and deliverance is necessary to move forward in life.

It was just a mistaken identity. I was chained to my trauma because I settled with my failures. I took a seat with my trauma and was even in a relationship with my trauma. I was so chained to my trauma; I stayed married to it for more than 25 years. It felt like all my failures, rejection, low self-esteem, guilt, shame, and embarrassment had me so chained, I couldn't break loose.

Despite choices you've made in the past, God sees you as fearfully and wonderfully made. You are good in his eyes and heart. Your mistakes will never change his mind concerning you. God's love for you is unconditional and everlasting. When you find his voice, it will connect you with a love that can't be compared to anything else. You will never find a love like the love of Jesus Christ. You can overcome trauma by the blood of Jesus Christ and the power of your testimony.

No, dear brothers and sisters, I have not achieved it, but I focus on this one thing: Forgetting the past and looking forward to what lies ahead, I press on to reach the end of the race and receive the heavenly prize for which God, through Christ Jesus, is calling us (Philippians 3:13-14 NLT).

There will always be obstacles and hurdles in in your life, but I am here to serve you notice that you must abandon what's behind you. Don't let anything cause you to look back. You must keep moving forward despite adversity, difficulty, or affliction. Don't deny your past, but also don't allow it to cripple you from moving forward.

Forget and abandon the guilt and shame that your past brought. Shame is just a strategy that makes you feel unworthy and stuck. It can block you from believing YOU are who God says YOU are. Shame can block you from seeing yourself properly and can trap you in a time, experience, feeling, or action. And when you lose focus and take our eyes off Christ, it can cause delays or you can trip, slip, and fall.

No matter how strong the wind gets, no matter the opposition we endure, we never give up on ourselves. We never come to a complete stop because we keep moving and keep our focus on all that lies ahead. The truth of who Christ says we are, is a truth that will set us free. We place our trust and dependency upon the Lord to give us our next steps…why?

BECAUSE GOD SAID SO!

But forget all that – it is nothing compared to what I am going to do. For I am about to do something new. See, I have already begun! Do you not see it? I will make a pathway through the wilderness. I will create rivers in the dry wasteland (Isaiah 43:18-19 NLT).

My testimony is one with many layers. It has layers of lies that I had to abandon. I am a new woman today who is no longer chained to what's behind me. I had to partner with God to understand that my identity was not in my experiences. My identity could only be found in him. I had to come into agreement with the One who created me and was pleased with what he created in me. So, for me there was no other choice.

I am in the next half of my life, and I am telling every lie that comes up; "That ain't what God said!" I'm walking with the sword of Truth in my hand (the Word of God). I'm not reducing who God says I am to make anyone feel comfortable. Don't mistake my freedom for arrogance. I'm walking with my head held high simply BECAUSE GOD SAID SO. As I am evolving, I am stepping into my purpose. I pray that every step I take empowers you to come into agreement with who God says YOU are.

Want to know what God says about you? Pick up the sword of truth and start slashing the lies that your trauma has told you. Get your papers, file for a divorce, and abandon what has kept you stagnant. It's a lie and that is my final answer.

Arise SONS and DAUGHTERS.

Arise KINGS and QUEENS.

Then help someone else ARISE.

MY PRAYER FOR YOU

If you openly declare that Jesus is Lord and believe in your heart that God raised him from the dead, you will be saved. For it is by believing in your heart that you are made right with God, and it is by openly declaring your faith that you are saved.

– Romans 10:9-10 NLT

I pray that after reading this book you have identified with the Father's love for you. God is ready to do for you what He has done for me and so many others. His hand, His heart and His love is reaching to pull you out of the pit. Nothing can or ever will separate us from the Love of Christ Jesus (Romans 8:38-39 NLT).

Father God in the mighty name of Jesus oh Great and mighty God that you are, I lift every reader of this book and I pray that He or she will find that their identity is found in you. Father, grant them your wisdom, your knowledge and understanding that you have loved them from the beginning, that no situation, or circumstance will ever change your love for them. Father God, I pray that this is the day that they choose you over their past, their trauma and their pain that they be found seeking you and searching for your voice that guides them out of darkness and into your marvelous light. I pray that their hope, trust, and dependency is found relying on you. I pray that they too will begin to see themselves as you see them, fearfully and wonderfully made. I pray that what has been shared has encouraged you and given you a hope to trust God and to try Him. God's entire nature is love and he has loved you so much that He chose His son to die for you. Amen

If you don't know Christ as your Lord and Savior and desire to know him and accept his salvation, it's very simple. Say the Salvation Prayer on the next page and receive Jesus Christ today!

SALVATION PRAYER

Dear Lord Jesus, I know that I am a sinner, and I ask for Your forgiveness. I believe you died on the cross for my sins and rose from the dead. I turn from my sins and invite You to come into my heart and life. I want to trust and follow You as my Lord and Savior. Amen.

NEXT STEPS

For whoever calls on the name of the LORD shall be saved. That if you confess with your mouth the Lord Jesus and believe in your heart that God has raised Him from the dead, you will be saved

– Romans 10:13

Salvation is a free gift from God and there is nothing you can do to deserve it. All you must do is receive it.

If you just prayed a sincere prayer of faith and you're wondering what to do next as a new Christian, here are a few suggestions:

- Tell someone about your decision. Find a brother or sister in Christ and let them know you decided to follow Christ.

- Talk to God daily. You don't have to be fancy about it. You can talk to God the same way you talk to a friend. There is no right or wrong way to talk to Him. You can pray with your eyes open or closed, sitting, or standing, anytime anywhere. The most important thing is to just be yourself.
- Find a church and get plugged in.

NOTES

Made in the USA
Middletown, DE
11 October 2022

12527418R00066